Claude Monet 1905

Thank you

Jean-Marie Toulgouat, Monet's step-great-grandson, who told us about the artist and showed us his family photographs

Claire Joyes, who wrote the book about Monet (which Mr. Bloom had), from which we learned so much

Philippe Piguet, another step-great-grandson, who had family photographs to show us and who read to us from Alice's and Blanche's diaries

Carlo Derkert, who read the manuscript, pointed out this and that, ate cakes, and discussed Impressionism with us

Jan Staël von Holstein, who showed us the Hotel Esmeralda and other important places

Madame C. Lindsey at the Claude Monet Museum in Giverny, who encouraged us in our work

Denise Moser and *Michel Carrière* at the French Embassy, who wrote so many letters of introduction for us

Jan Sundfeldt, who helped us with difficult French words

Michèle Bruel and *Canelle,* who make the Hotel Esmeralda such a lovely place to stay

Bo Åkermark, who told us about Paris's second-oldest tree

Monet's paintings

(Book page; year painted; where painting is now)
- 3 1899. Musée d'Orsay, Paris
- 8 About 1903. Musée Marmottan, Paris
- 10 1872. Musée Marmottan, Paris
- 22 Top of the page: 1899. Musée d'Orsay, Paris
  Bottom of the page: 1919. Musée Marmottan, Paris
- 23 Top of the page: 1899. Musée d'Orsay, Paris
  Bottom of the page: 1923. Musée Marmottan, Paris
- 25 1907. Musée d'Art et d'Industrie, Saint-Étienne
- 33 1916–1926. Musée de l'Orangerie, Paris
- 37 1873. Musée d'Orsay, Paris
- 38 1879. Musée d'Orsay, Paris
- 39 1887. Musée d'Orsay, Paris
- 43 1897. Museum of Fine Arts, Boston

End papers: 1905. Museum of Fine Arts, Boston

The photographs

Front cover: Collection Sirot / Angel, Paris
- 1 Collection Musée Marmottan, Paris
- 4 Maria Brännström, Umeå
- 16–17 Christina Björk, Stockholm
- 19 Editions d'Art Lys, Versailles
- 24 Collection Piguet, Paris
- 26–27 Christina Björk, Stockholm
- 29 International Museum of Photography, George Eastman House, New York
- 33 Collection Musée Marmottan, Paris
- 35 Collection Toulgouat, Giverny
- 36 Collection Piguet, Paris
- 38 Collection Toulgouat, Giverny
- 39 Collection Toulgouat, Giverny
- 40–41 Collection Toulgouat, Giverny
- 44–45 Nisse Peterson, Stockholm (who also took the photos of pressed leaves)

Back cover: Nicolina Ringqvist

Text copyright © 1985, 2012 by Christina Björk
Cover and internal illustrations © 1985, 2012 by Lena Anderson
Translation © 1987, 2012 by Joan Sandin
Cover and internal design © Christina Björk and Lena Anderson

Published by Sourcebooks Jabberwocky, an imprint of Sourcebooks, Inc.
P.O. Box 4410, Naperville, Illinois 60567-4410
(630) 961-3900
Fax: (630) 961-2168
www.jabberwockykids.com

Originally published in Sweden in 1985 by Rabén & Sjögren.

Library of Congress Cataloging-in-Publication data is on file with the publisher.

Oceanic Graphic Printing, Kowloon, Hong Kong, China
Date of Production: March 2020
Run Number: 5018342

Printed and bound in China.
OGP 10 9 8

Linnea
in Monet's Garden

Christina Björk & Lena Anderson

sourcebooks
jabberwocky

Just think—I've been in a famous artist's garden! And I've been in Paris! My friend Mr. Bloom was with me. In fact, the whole thing was actually his idea. But maybe I should start at the beginning.

I *love* flowers (I'm even named after a flower). And that's how Mr. Bloom is, too. He's my upstairs neighbor. Mr. Bloom used to be a gardener. He's retired now, which is good because it means he has lots of time to spend with me.

When I go visit him, I like to look in a book that Mr. Bloom has about the French artist *Claude Monet*. Monet loved flowers, too. He painted lots of pictures of them. Probably his best known flower paintings are his pictures of water lilies.

There are reproductions of Monet's paintings in Mr. Bloom's book and old photographs of the artist, his wife, *Alice,* and all eight children. There are also pictures of their garden and the big pink house where they lived over a hundred years ago.

The longer Monet lived there, the more flowers he planted. Later he used the garden in his paintings. He even had a pond put into the garden so that he could have water lilies to paint.

The painter Claude Monet in 1913

1

I've looked so often at Mr. Bloom's book that sometimes I think I know them all—Monet, Alice, and the eight children. And I almost feel that I've been in the big pink house. I can pretend that I have, anyway. Mostly I pretend that I'm standing on the Japanese bridge looking at the lily pond. One day I told Mr. Bloom about it.

"It's possible to *really* stand on that bridge," said Mr. Bloom.

"You mean it's still there?" I asked.

"I read in the paper that they were collecting money to restore the house and garden. They had become completely run-down and overgrown.

But now they look almost exactly as they did when Monet lived there, and they have turned into a museum. Anybody can go there and look."

"But Monet and the children can't still be around?"

"No," said Mr. Bloom. "They died a long time ago, just like your great-great-grandfather and his children."

"But what about the garden— how does someone get there?"

"First one would have to get to Paris," said Mr. Bloom.

"Oh!" I said. "That's a long way away."

"It's a long way," said Mr. Bloom, "but it's not *impossible*."

Monet, Alice, and the eight children

The Japanese bridge that Monet painted

Paris

And just think—everything was formally arranged so that I could go to Paris with Mr. Bloom. We went in August because Mr. Bloom said the water lilies would be best then.

Our hotel was called the *Esmeralda*. It was tiny and old, but Mr. Bloom thought that it was probably the loveliest hotel in the whole city of Paris. It was right on the River Seine, which flows through all of Paris.

From my window, I could see *Notre-Dame* Cathedral. That is the city's most famous church. The book *The Hunchback of Notre-Dame* takes place there. Mr. Bloom hadn't read the book,

but he had seen the film. It's about a terribly ugly bell ringer named *Quasimodo* and a beautiful gypsy named *Esmeralda*.

The hotel is named after Esmeralda, of course, and in the hall there is a painting of her dancing with her little pet goat, *Djali*. There is also a red couch in the hall, where the hotel's dog, *Canelle,* always sits. The cats *Mona* and *Lisa* lie in the armchairs, but *Tiger* prefers to sit in the window, staring and purring.

Mr. Bloom discovered that the house was built in 1640. At that time there was a secret passage under the house, leading down to the river.

The city's second-oldest tree

The walls were made of uneven stones, and there were ancient beams in the ceiling. But the furniture wasn't that old. It was only about as old as Monet.

In front of the hotel is a park that belongs to the church of *Saint-Julien le Pauvre* (which means St. Julius the Poor). The city's second-oldest tree grows there, supported by a cement pillar. It is a Robinia

(or false Acacia) which came all the way from America in a basket and was planted there in 1681. It still has fresh green leaves, even though it's more than three hundred years old! I couldn't reach up to them, so I took a leaf from another tree in the park to press in my travel diary.

There were so many interesting things to look at from my window, especially the dogs. In Paris, lots of dogs go out by themselves. Canelle knows them all. Her boyfriend, *Baskerville*, belongs to the English bookshop around the corner.

My first day in Paris, I saw a very old and elegant gentleman walking down the street. All of a sudden, two enormous dogs ran right into him. It looked as if they were going to knock him over! Then Canelle ran out to join them. Soon all three dogs were jumping all over the poor man.

I found out later that the biggest dog belongs to the old man. He goes walking there several times a day and thinks it's fun to be almost knocked over by the dogs. He started saying hello to me when he noticed me watching from my window.

"Imitate the old man with the dog," I say to Mr. Bloom some-times. And when he does his imitation, I laugh so much that I almost fall over.

But now on to the most important part—Monet and his flowers.

At the Museum

Our first day in Paris, we took the *Métro* (the underground train) to a museum called the *Marmottan*. Many of Monet's paintings are there. It's one thing to see them in a book, but something quite different to see the real thing. I know that now.

The Monet paintings at the Marmottan used to belong to the artist's youngest son, *Michel*. When Michel was eighty-eight years old, he was run over and killed. Since he didn't have any children of his own, he left his father's paintings to the museum.

Most of the pictures are hanging in large rooms downstairs. There we discovered that Monet had not only painted water lilies; he had also painted steam engines, churches, mountains, the sea, and people. There were snow paintings, too.

"But *this one* is nice, Mr. Bloom," I said.

We were standing in front of a painting with two white water lilies. I stepped a little closer to the picture and looked at it. It was then I noticed that the lilies were nothing but blobs and blotches of paint.

The water lilies are beautiful from a distance...

But when I stepped away again, they turned into real water lilies floating in a pond—magic!

"How could he know how to paint like that?" I asked Mr. Bloom. "He had to stand near the canvas to paint, so how did he know what it would look like from a distance?"

"Let me think," said Mr. Bloom.

"Maybe he tied the brush to a long stick," I suggested.

"I don't think so," said Mr. Bloom. "I think that he had practiced painting like that for such a long time that he knew exactly what to do."

. . . but splotchy when you get up close!

9

The Impressionist

"Come over here, Linnea," said Mr. Bloom. "You have to look at this."

"Why?" I asked, because I hadn't even noticed *that* little picture before. It was a seascape with some small boats at sunrise. The sun looked like an orange blob.

"This is an important painting in history," explained Mr. Bloom. "It's called *Impression—Sunrise*. Monet painted his *impression* of sunlight reflected in the water. After that, the art critics started calling Monet an Impressionist in the newspapers. And they didn't mean it as a compliment. They thought painting impressions of the moment was a waste of time. Paintings should be precise, and carefully done. They should be a little gray and dark, too."

At that time, almost no one liked Monet's paintings. Ooh, what a lot of blobs, people said. They thought they looked messy, sloppy, and unfinished. And such loud colors! But Monet didn't care what they said. He didn't want to mix black into his colors. He wanted to paint his impressions with bright dabs of color that would shine and sparkle on the canvas and make it come alive. And Monet saw that it wasn't only water that sparkled. Leaves could also reflect the sun, and skin, clothes, and even stone walls could shimmer.

But it was water that Monet thought was the most fun to paint. What color is water, actually? One moment it looks blue, the next moment it's white. Those were little moments that Monet tried to capture in paint. But it wasn't easy. Those moments disappear so quickly, and it takes so many of them to paint a picture.

Upstairs in the museum were paintings by Monet's artist friends. The critics also called them

Impressionists. One was named *Pissarro*. Some others were *Renoir* and *Sisley* and *Berthe Morisot*. Berthe was the only woman in their group. In those days, women who wanted to be painters usually ended up keeping house for male artists or becoming their models.

Monet and most of his friends were poor. There are letters in the museum that Monet wrote begging to borrow money for food, rent, and paints. Imagine! Today people pay a fortune for a Monet painting.

In the museum gift shop, I found a poster of *my* Monet (the one with the white water lilies). Luckily, it didn't cost a fortune. We went downstairs and looked at the real painting again. Then I sat down for a while in front of the painting with the little boat.

"Do you think the boat is still there?" I asked Mr. Bloom.

"We'll see tomorrow," he said.

To Giverny

Early the next morning, we took the Métro to the train station called *Gare Saint-Lazare*. I was a little disappointed that it didn't have a steam engine as in Monet's painting *Gare Saint-Lazare*.

It took only an hour to get there, following the River Seine. We passed beaches, boats, docks, houses, and lots of "hanging trees" (weeping willows, hanging over the water) and "high-rise trees" (by that I mean poplars). We got off in the town of *Vernon*. At the station there were bicycles for rent. You could ride to the village of *Giverny*, where Monet's house is.

"Do you have any child seats for the bicycles?" asked Mr. Bloom.

"I'm sorry, sir, there are no child seats," said the man at the bicycle rental.

"I can ride by myself," I said.

"When you're older," said Mr. Bloom. "Today we're taking a taxi."

"Oh no, not a taxi!" I said.

"But first we have to buy some things for our picnic," said Mr. Bloom.

"Oh no, not a picnic!" I said.

But then we found a nice bakery,

where we bought a *baguette*. And what a wonderful cheese shop there was! How could we ever decide which to buy? Finally we chose a small goat cheese and a somewhat larger cow's milk cheese (in case I didn't like the goat cheese). In another shop we bought pâté, tomatoes, and nectarines. We got some mineral water, plus a small bottle of wine for Mr. Bloom.

At the square, we found a taxi that drove us to Giverny.

"Mr. Bloom, look!" I cried. "Look up there! You can see the pink house!"

And then we were inside! Mr. Bloom paid the entrance fees and left our picnic basket with the lady at the door. I ran ahead of him out into the garden.

"Mr. Bloom," I said, "it doesn't look anything like I thought it would."

"It doesn't?" said Mr. Bloom, a little worried.

"No," I said, "because I never could have imagined all *this*. There are *so* many flowers!"

If we could have looked at the garden from above, it probably would have looked like stripes—stripes of gravel paths and rows of flower beds in different colors. Mr. Bloom knew the names of almost all the flowers. In the blue row there were flax flowers, bluebells, and delphiniums. In the pink row there were foxgloves, hollyhocks, and roses.

By the widest path there were nasturtiums, their orange flowers practically covering the gravel path. It was as if the flowers on one side of the path were trying to crawl over to the flowers on the other side.

A couple of the rows had flowers of all different colors. Some were so tall that they hung out over the path. I could squat down and see flowers all around me.

Next we looked at the pigeon house and the turkey pen. Can you think of a funnier-looking bird than a turkey?

Small blue flax flowers

Foxglove

Hydrangea

Busy Lizzie at the foot of a tree

We both had our cameras with us,
I had my sketchbook, but should I
look, draw, or photograph?
A cat followed us around.

Hibiscus

Poppies

Hydrangea again

One of the many, many roses

Monet's kitchen

You can go inside the pink house and look at Monet's bedroom (but not the children's) and the old studio and the yellow dining room. Best of all is the blue kitchen. One of the chairs must have been made for a child. I tried sitting in it when nobody was looking.

You aren't allowed to take pictures inside the house, but luckily there are postcards of all the different rooms.

I sat out on the back steps, as Monet's family used to do.

"We are sitting here and pretending that we are Monet's family," I wrote home on a postcard. "The garden is really nice. The flowers are bigger than the ones at home, except for the balsams. Now we're going down to look at the lily pond. Love from Linnea + a cat."

A little cupboard for fresh eggs

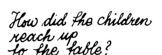

How did the children reach up to the table?

19

Finally, the Japanese Bridge!

After we looked at both the garden and the house, the best part was still to come: the lily pond. We crossed the garden and went through a tunnel under the main road.

"Oh, look, Mr. Bloom!" I cried. "There's the Japanese bridge!"

And when at last we were standing on the bridge, it was so thrilling that there were tears in my eyes. (And in Mr. Bloom's. I'm sure I saw a few.)

"What was it I said?" said Mr. Bloom. "It *was* possible!"

"That's right. And now we're really here," I said. "It could never be more now than right now."

"If we don't come back another time, that is," said Mr. Bloom.

We looked down at all the water lilies—red, pink, and white. A wisteria climbed the bridge.

We saw some big fish swimming around in the water. Mr. Bloom said they were carp. They help keep the pond clean by eating insects and plants.

Inside a bamboo thicket, there it was—the little green boat! It looked almost like the picture in the Marmottan Museum.

"Let's say we can't look at the bridge again until we've gone around to the other side," I said.

A wisteria leaf from the bridge

"Why?" asked Mr. Bloom.

"So we can get our own *impression* of the bridge, just like Monet," I said.

But by the time we got to the other side, all of my impressions were forgotten. A bird had flown by and a friendly man in a checked jacket had said hello. Oh well, I guess I wouldn't make much of an Impressionist. Neither would Mr. Bloom.

But Monet *practiced* capturing impressions. Every day, he studied his bridge. He discovered that it looked different depending on the time of day and the weather. Sunlight made the difference.

Monet painted many pictures of the bridge. He would take several canvases with him, painting a little on each one as the sun rose higher in the sky. People thought he was strange, painting the same bridge over and over again.

When Monet was an old man, he got a cataract and became almost blind. He kept on painting anyway, but his pictures were almost all red. When he finally let a doctor operate on his eyes, all the other colors returned to his paintings.

Here is how Monet painted

Look how he painted the

the bridge in 1899. This bridge is also from 1899.

bridge in 1919... ...and in 1923, when he could barely see.

I took out my sketchbook and decided to draw just *one* water lily. I thought it would be too hard to draw the *whole* pond with the clouds reflected on the water *at the same time* as the seaweed under the water.

I wasn't satisfied with my water lily. But then, Monet was never satisfied with his pictures either. Sometimes he burned a pile of paintings in the garden.

Stepdaughter Blanche helped Monet carry his painting things. The little girl in the foreground is named Nitia. She was the daughter of Blanche's sister Germaine.

Claude Monet 1907

There were lots of little bluish-green bridges in the garden.

Just think - the boat was still there!
Is it the same one that's in the painting?

Mr. Bloom told me that Monet bought the land where the lily pond is when he was fifty-three years old. Three years earlier he had been able to afford the house. People had *finally* started to like his paintings.

I took pictures of the pond from lots of different angles.

This is the impression the water lilies made on my camera.

When Monet Was Old

Under an arch of climbing roses, we found the bench where Monet used to sit and look at his lily pond. Naturally, we went over and sat down, just as he used to.

"Tell me about when Monet was old," I said.

"It was then that he got his great idea," said Mr. Bloom. "He started work on the biggest pictures he had ever painted. They would cover the walls of two huge round halls.

"Monet had to build a new studio so as to have room for the pictures. He painted and painted for the last ten years of his life. When the panels were covered with paint, he started to paint over parts of the pictures and make changes. As usual, he wasn't satisfied. Finally his best friend told him he had to stop before he destroyed the paintings, that at that moment they were already masterpieces. Monet didn't think so, but he did stop making changes."

"Are the masterpieces still around?" I asked Mr. Bloom.

"The Water Lily Rooms are in the *Orangerie* in Paris," said Mr. Bloom. "That used to be the king's greenhouse, but now it's a museum. But the rooms have been closed for repairs."

"I hope they've opened them again," I said.

This picture of Monet sitting on the bench was taken the last summer of his life. The paintings were finished by then, but he didn't want to let go of them. They were still hanging in his studio when he died. He lived to be eighty-six years old.

Picnic by the River Ru

"Mr. Bloom, we forgot something,"

"Our lunch!" said Mr. Bloom.

"And I'm *starving!*" I said.

"This would be a good place for a picnic," said Mr. Bloom, "right here by Monet's bench."

We went up to the pink house to get our picnic basket. But there we found out that picnicking in the garden was not allowed. People would just litter and make a mess, explained the lady.

"Well then, we'll find a good place outside the garden," said Mr. Bloom.

"Not as good as by Monet's bench," I said.

But we did find a good place, by the River Ru, just where it flows into the garden.

"What a feast!" said Mr. Bloom. "Could it be any better than this?"

As it turned out, the goat cheese wasn't all that bad, but the cow's milk cheese was much better. (Mr. Bloom

thought just the opposite, which was lucky for me.) The pâté was also good, especially with the long *baguette*.

After lunch I lay on my back in the grass and watched the clouds sailing by in the sky.

"Don't fall asleep now," said Mr. Bloom. "Soon we have to call a taxi so we won't miss our train in Vernon."

I slept all the way on the train back to Paris. I didn't see a single bend of the river.

Back at the hotel, I went right to bed without even waiting to see the old man and the dog.

The Masterpiece!

The museum in Paris with the most Impressionist paintings is called the *Musée d'Orsay*.

When we arrived, there was a big crowd in front of the entrance.

"We can't stand there and wait," said Mr. Bloom.

"Then let's go and see if the masterpiece museum is open," I said.

We took the Metro to the Orangerie.

But we didn't see any arrows or signs pointing out the way to Monet's water lilies.

"Sorry, but the Water Lily Rooms are closed for repairs," said the lady at the door. "But they will open again next month, and you are welcome to come back then."

"The thing is," Mr. Bloom explained, "this little girl and I have

Monet painting the giant water lilies

come a long way to see the water lilies, and we have to go home the day after tomorrow. Can't you make an exception?"

"Unfortunately not," said the lady. "The rooms are closed to the public."

And when she said that, Mr. Bloom looked so sad that I burst into tears.

"Oh, dear!" said the lady. "Let me see if something can be done."

After a long time, she returned and winked at us.

"My boss has made an exception for you, sir, and for the young lady. Come along, discreetly, so none of the other visitors will notice."

So that's how we ended up right in the *middle* of the masterpiece itself. Good thing that I started crying at the entrance.

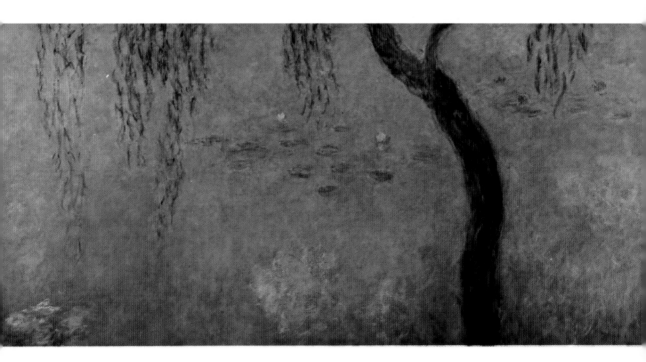

We Meet a Great-Grandson

"Tomorrow is our last day in Paris," said Mr. Bloom.

"Oh, no," I said. "It's going too fast!"

"I agree," said Mr. Bloom. "That's why we'll have to do something *extra* special. Shall we go up the *Eiffel* Tower?"

"Maybe," I said. "Too bad we've already been to Giverny."

"You can do the same thing twice," said Mr. Bloom. "If it's something *extra* special, that is."

Mr. Bloom counted our money. Yes, there was enough for train tickets, taxi, and museum.

So the next day we were back in Monet's garden again. When we were standing by the pigeon house, a man in a checked jacket came up to us.

"So you've come back again," he said.

"How did you know that?" asked Mr. Bloom.

"I recognize the girl in the straw hat," said the man.

And guess who it was! Monet's step-great-grandson! His name was *Jean-Marie Toulgouat*, and he was a painter, too. But he painted much stranger pictures than Monet's, he said. He lived in the village, and when he was little, he used to play here in the garden.

"Tell us about Monet and Alice and the eight children," I begged.

"Both Monet and Alice died before I was born," said Jean-Marie. "The one who ran everything was Alice's daughter Blanche, my grandmother's sister. All of us children loved her because she was so nice. I remember how surprised she looked once when she saw a sail crossing the garden. But it was only I who had rigged up a bed sheet on the little boat in the lily pond."

Jean-Marie showed us some old photographs of his relatives. And guess what—it was his wife who wrote the book about Monet that Mr. Bloom has!

Now it's time for me to explain a little about Monet's big family, because they were not at all like an ordinary family. Some of it is in Mr. Bloom's book, and some Jean-Marie told us there in the garden.

Monet's large and unusual family, together in
the garden in 1886. The youngest boys, Jean-Pierre
and _Michel_, when they were eight and nine years old.

Monet's Story

Monet decided early in life that he wanted to be a painter. But his family thought he should work in their grocery shop instead. The only one who supported Monet was his aunt, *Madame Lecadre*. She had been a painter herself, and she gave him a little money so he could study art in Paris.

In Paris, Monet made many artist friends, just as poor as he was. He had a girlfriend named *Camille* who had dark hair and dark, serious eyes. Monet painted her often—four, five women in the same picture, and all of them were Camille.

Camille and Monet had a son, *Jean*. After that they got married (although Monet's father was against it).

Monet had two friends who were not poor, *Alice* and *Ernest Hochedé*. Ernest owned several exclusive department stores in Paris, and he bought paintings from Monet for his summer palace.

Monet in 1880

Camille and little Jean (six years old) take a walk in a poppy field. Not a single blob really looks like a poppy, but together they give the _impression_ of a poppy field!
(BEHIND THEM IS ANOTHER MOTHER AND CHILD; MAYBE THEY ARE CAMILLE AND JEAN TOO)

Monet's painting of Camille after her death

Sorrows and Worries

Suddenly it came out that Ernest didn't have as much money as everybody thought. His department stores went bankrupt, and all the paintings had to be sold. Ernest left the country. Alice and their five children had to fend for themselves! There was even one more on the way!

Alice sold all her jewelry and started sewing clothes for her rich friends. Her son *Jean-Pierre* was born on the train when Alice was on her way to visit her sister.

That summer, Monet and Camille decided to rent a summer house, together with Alice and her children. When Camille and Monet's son Michel was born, there were eight children in the house. But there was no money. Camille and Alice had only one nice dress, which they took turns wearing.

Camille developed tuberculosis and died. Monet became depressed. He couldn't paint any longer, he was so unhappy. Alice had to take care of him, the two babies, and the other six children. It was a good thing they all had Alice.

They ended up staying in the summer house for several years, because they couldn't afford to live in Paris. Monet started painting again. One day, when he had succeeded in selling some of his paintings, he took the train to look for a better place to live. In those days the train passed the village of Giverny, and there he saw his dream house, the pink one. And guess what! They could rent it!

The whole family moved in. Monet started at once to make changes in the garden. He got rid of all the well-trimmed hedges and planted flowers instead, plus a large vegetable garden to feed them all. The children had to weed and water it every evening.

Germaine kept pigeons, and Suzanne was the one who took care of the turkeys. Blanche loved to paint,

Alice

and she followed Monet, helping him carry all the canvases. No matter what the weather or time of day, Blanche went along and helped him.

In the River *Epte*, the children used to row and fish and swim. Jean and Jacques caught frogs. One day they caught sixty of them. (In France, people eat frog legs.)

Jean-Pierre and Michel collected wild plants and pressed them. They made their own book about plants, and it was published. Once they managed to cross an Oriental poppy with a wild one. The new poppy was called *papaver Moneti* in Latin!

The youngest children, Jean-Pierre and Michel, always played together.

Germaine, Suzanne, and Blanche fishing in the river Epte

Blanche (standing) at a picnic. The older girl on the right is Jean-Marie's mother, Lili.

Sometimes they went ice-skating on the river Epte.

In the village of Giverny, people thought that Monet and his family were a strange bunch. Was painting pictures any real job? And what about a whole family going out with parasols and picnic baskets and carts just to eat. Nobody had ever done anything like that in their village before. The only one who seemed normal in that family was the lady of the house. But then she was living with Monet without being married to him.

But Alice couldn't marry Monet. Ernest refused to divorce her.

After a few years, Ernest died. Alice and Monet arranged for him to be buried in Giverny. A year later, Alice and Monet could finally get married.

In the meantime, Monet's paintings had started to become famous. Art dealers came to Giverny all the way from America. Monet thought it

was terrible that his pictures would be taken so far away. But he needed the money, for now they had lots of guests, a cook, an assistant cook, and (best of all, according to the children) six gardeners.

When Monet was pleased with his paintings, then the whole household was happy. But when he was not pleased, everyone suffered. Monet's views and moods ruled the house. Lunch was to be served at exactly twelve o'clock, even if the children had to leave school early. The boys' professions and the girls' husbands had to be approved by Monet. Michel did not get to be an inventor, and poor Germaine did not get to marry her boyfriend. Blanche was luckier. She was allowed to marry her stepbrother Jean! And Suzanne got to marry an American painter named *Theodore Butler.*

Jean-Marie and Grandfather Butler painting.

Suzanne had two children, *Jim* and *Lili*. But tragedy struck the family again. Suzanne died. Her children moved in with Monet, where Suzanne's older sister, Marthe, took care of them. After a few years, Theodore married Marthe.

Many years later, Monet's own beloved Alice died, as well as his son Jean. Monet became so depressed again that he was unable to paint. It wasn't until Blanche moved back to the pink house that things got better. She dragged Monet and all his equipment out into the garden. Soon they were standing there painting again, just like old times. (But Blanche's paintings never became as famous as Monet's.)

That was the story of the Monet family. But I forgot one thing: when Lili grew up, she had a son named Jean-Marie, the one Mr. Bloom and I are talking with in Monet's garden!

"Imagine having such a famous father," I said.

"And so strict," said Mr. Bloom.

"I think the girls made out best," said Jean-Marie. "The boys had it much harder. Think of poor Michel, the one who wanted to be an inventor. He was a good painter, too, but he never dared show his paintings to anyone as long as he lived."

Jean-Marie went along with us to the graveyard in the village. There we stood a long time, reading all the names on the gravestones: Claude, Alice, Ernest, Suzanne, Blanche, Marthe, Michel.

Sunrise on the Seine

The next day we had to leave Paris. Mr. Bloom woke me up at six o'clock!

"If you get up right now, we'll have time to see one more thing," he said.

"No…what…what is it now?" I said.

"Sunrise on the Seine," said Mr. Bloom.

"Go by yourself," I said from under the blanket.

But I ended up going with him after all. It was foggy and damp outside. We crossed the bridge to the island called *Île de la Cité*. Way over on the west end of the island was a weeping willow tree, its branches hanging over the river. In the distance we could see the Eiffel Tower. At that moment, the first rays of the sun appeared, warming us.

"I'm thinking of a certain painting," said Mr. Bloom. "One of those in the book."

"I know which one you mean," I said. "It's the second most misty of the sunrise-on-the-Seine paintings."

A leaf from the weeping willow tree

Home Again

It's lucky that there are some good things about a trip's being over—coming home and telling everybody about it, for example. And seeing how all the pictures turned out.

"We forgot to take a picture of the old man with the dog," I said.

"But I have one of Canelle," said Mr. Bloom.

"Do your imitation of the old man with the dog," I said.

And when Mr. Bloom did it, I laughed until I fell over.

I showed Mr. Bloom my bulletin

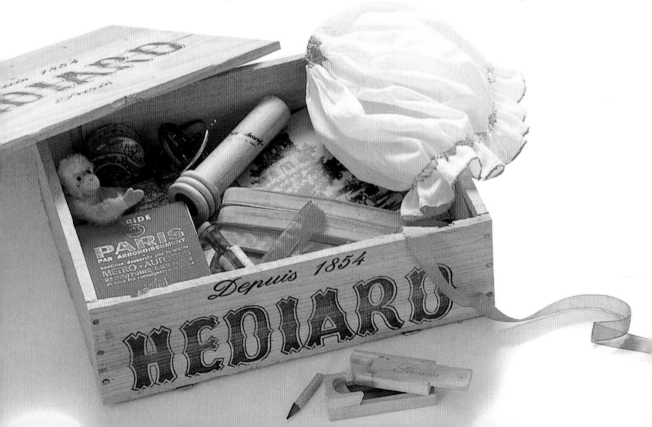

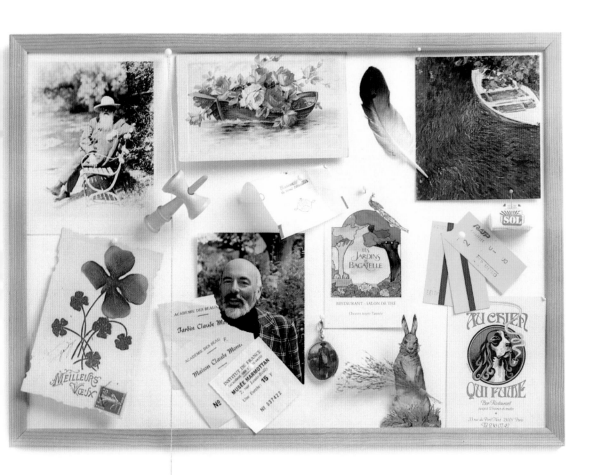

board, where I've pinned up post-cards and tickets from our trip, a pigeon feather, and a photo of Jean-Marie.

I have some other things in a wooden box that I found in a trash can in Paris: a little monkey, a nightcap, a hundred meters of pink satin ribbon (all of that I bought for next to nothing at the flea market in Paris), and a red book of city maps.

Almost everybody knows now that I've been in Monet's garden and that I've been in Paris! But when they ask, "How was the Eiffel Tower?" I answer: "We actually didn't go. We had far more important things to see than that."

Museums

The Claude Monet Museum (www.fondation-monet.fr/uk) in Giverny is open every day from April 1 to November 1. The house and the garden can be seen from 9:30 a.m. to 6 p.m. Take the *Rouen* train from the *Gare Saint-Lazare* in Paris. (Travel time, forty-five minutes.) Get off in Vernon. Rent a bicycle at the station, go by shuttle bus, or take a taxi. Signs show the way. By car from Paris, take A 13, exit *Bonnières*. It's 69 km from *Notre-Dame*.

Musée d'Art Américain, rue Claude Monet, Giverny. They have paintings by American artists painting in Monet's time.

The Marmottan (www.marmottan .com) in Paris is located at 2 rue Louis-Boilly. Métro station: *La Muette*. Open every day except Monday from 10 a.m. to 6 p.m. and until 8 p.m. on Tuesdays.

Musée d'Orsay (www.musee-orsay.fr), open every day except Monday from 9:30 a.m. to 6 p.m. Thursdays to 9:45 p.m. Métro station: *Solferino*. Very fine bookshop with many children's books.

The Orangerie in the Tuileries Gardens. (www.musee-orangerie .fr) Métro station: *Concorde*. Open every day except Tuesday from 12:30 p.m. to 7 p.m., 9 p.m. on Fridays. Monet's water lilies are downstairs. The permanent Impressionist collection is on the first floor. Linnea especially liked Renoir's son dressed up in a red clown costume. Mr. Bloom preferred Cézanne's little lemon painting.

In the **Tuileries Garden** you can rent a boat and go sailing in the pond, ride a pony, and eat ice cream.

Île de la Cité. Go to *Notre-Dame*

More Things to Do in Paris

Cathedral and climb the 255 steps to the terrace for a view of Paris. Linnea took pictures of the funny devil statues there. Have the guide show you where the bell ringer of *Notre-Dame* hung out. There are twenty-two more steps up to the bell tower. The bell itself weighs 28,660 pounds (the clapper, 110 pounds) and can be heard for six kilometers. Eight men are needed to ring it, but now the job is done by a machine. Ten (or more) people can go into the bell and listen carefully to the sound. Don't forget to leave a tip in the pot for the guides before you leave.

The Flower Market. Linnea visited the flower market near Notre-Dame bridge and bought a bouquet to take back to the hotel room. Some days there is a bird market there, too.

Shakespeare & Co. is the bookshop where Canelle's boyfriend, Baskerville, lived. The address is 37 rue de la Bûcherie. Wonderful children's book department on the first floor, where you can lie down on velvet mattresses and read all the books.

The Bagatelle Gardens, in the *Bois de Boulogne*, is a rose garden. Every year a rose competition is held there. When Linnea visited the garden, number 18 Meilland had won the prize for the best-smelling rose. Linnea took pictures of the boy statue Pan and the lower right part of the gardens, just inside the entrance.

The Flea Market. Linnea was there. You get off at the Métro station *Porte de Montreuil*. A larger version is at *Port de Clignancourt*. Both of them are best to visit on Saturday or Sunday morning.

Books

Claude Monet: Life and Art by Paul Hayes Tucker. New Haven, CT: Yale University Press, 1998.

Claude Monet: Life at Giverny by Claire Joyes. London: Thames & Hudson, 1985. This is the book Mr. Bloom was reading. It's out of print, but you could find it in the library.

The Hunchback of Notre-Dame by Victor Hugo. A classic adventure. You may have seen it as Disney's animated movie.

Monet, or, the Triumph of Impressionism by Daniel Wildenstein. Cologne: Taschen, 2010.

Monet's Table by Claire Joyes. New York: Simon & Schuster, 1990. A big beautiful book about Monet, his family, and the food they ate (with recipes). It's a little expensive, but you can borrow it at the library.